# FINGERPRINTS ON LIGHT

## Jan Owen

*For Les
with warm regards
Jan
16th Dec '90*

Also by Jan Owen
BOY WITH A TELESCOPE

*Promotion of this title has been assisted by
the South Australian Government through
the Department for the Arts.*

 *Angus & Robertson Publishers'
creative writing programme is
assisted by the Australia Council,
the Federal Government's arts
funding and advisory body.*

ANGUS & ROBERTSON PUBLISHERS

*Unit 4, Eden Park, 31 Waterloo Road,
North Ryde, NSW, Australia 2113;
16 Golden Square, London W1R 4BN,
United Kingdom*

*This book is copyright.
Apart from any fair dealing for the
purposes of private study, research,
criticism or review, as permitted
under the Copyright Act, no part may
be reproduced by any process without
written permission. Inquiries should
be addressed to the publishers.*

*First published in Australia
by Angus & Robertson Publishers in 1990*

*Copyright © Jan Owen 1990*

*National Library of Australia
Cataloguing-in-publication data.*

*Owen, Jan, 1940–
Fingerprints on light.
ISBN 0 207 16582 3.
I. Title.
A821.3*

*Typeset in Palatino by Best-set Typesetter Ltd.
Printed in Australia by Australian Print Group,*

For my mother, Eva May Sincock
And in memory of my father, John Barnes Sincock

# ACKNOWLEDGEMENTS

Some of these poems have appeared in *The Adelaide Review, The Age, The Anglo-Welsh Review, Antipodes, Australian Poetry 1988, Fine Line, Friendly Street Poetry Reader No 11, Honest Ulsterman, Island Magazine, Kiwi and Emu, Kunapipi, Linq, Luna, Mattara* anthologies *An Inflection of Silence* and *The International Terminal, Meanjin, New Welsh Review, Other Poetry, Phoenix, Planet, Poetry Wales, Prairie Schooner, Prospice, Quadrant, Scarp, Southern Review, Span, Studio, Verse* and *Westerly*. Some have been broadcast by the ABC and by 5UV.

I am grateful to the Literature Board of the Australia Council, and to the South Australian Department for the Arts for the financial assistance which enabled me to write the poems in this collection.

# CONTENTS

**DOORSTEPS**
Digging Potatoes  2
Bread  3
Dividend  4
Stained Glass  5
Planting Seeds  6
The Outside Lavatory  8
Beetles  9
Gloves I Have Known  11
Loquats and Lacquerware  12
Old Soldiers  13
Touchdown  14
Day Trip  15
Group Portrait with Fireworks  16
Mortgage  17
Level Crossing  18
Rheomode  19

**EARTH-STAR**
Morning Song  22
Red Carnations  23
Fungus  24
Blackberries and Walnuts  25
Trees  26
*The Rowan to Dance  26*
*The Cherry Tree  26*

*The Red Gum  27*
*Smoke  27*
Calendar  28

**CRYSTAL FORESTS**

Touchstone  38

*Agates  38*
*Malachite  38*
*Amethyst Crystals  39*
*Fossil  40*
*Tektites  41*

Footprints  42
More on the Dinosaur  43
Fern  44

**PATHWAYS**

Write to Me at Rochefort  46
Hotel  56
Metro  58
Tower  59
Town  60
Kafenio  61
Room  62
Bridge  63

**ZIPPERS**

Watching the Battle from Afar  66
Domestibilia  67

*Thimble  67*

*Safety-pin 67*
*Zippers 68*
*Coat-hangers 68*
Alphabet 69
Still Life with Coffee Pot 70
Pan-pipes 71
Saxophone 72

# DOORSTEPS

# Digging Potatoes

My grandfather turned the earth
all morning long in the skittery autumn sun
on the weedy patch by the stable wall,
stacking unsteady pyramids
of dirty dimpled knees in the bonfire air
while the tame-tease willy wagtail
skimmed the flung-up clods
and thought me a rival for witchetty grubs.
It seems a sort of music now —
the shining edge of the spade descending bass
grounded the wagtail's flight
from shrill arpeggios after gnats
to a treble skirl of black and white,
a quick wing trill.
I was an interloper
set to disrupt the rhythm of work
between the man and bird.
"I can spell 'rhubarb' and hop two hundred
and stand on my head!"
He stopped and drove the spade in hard
to lean and look me over a while.
So much brown warmth, I feel it still —
brown earth and spuds, brown overalls, brown skin,
and his long freckled Cornish face concealing a smile.

# Bread

A "Whoa!" and a stamp and a snort meant the baker's cart.
We followed our noses to the gate

and the yeasty air round the dapper piebald horse
who clipped one house ahead as a matter of course

while Mr Jarvis ran his basket in.
We rode on the running board and hoped for a bun,

squashed or undersized with the icing missed.
At the corner, Mr Jarvis would entrust

to our angelic smiles the warm joined loaves.
Behind the jasmine bush we'd pull them in halves

and peel out strips and eat them fast;
the hollowed ends were steamy caves of taste.

We pushed in while our mother sawed it up
for doorsteps of bread and jam on the back doorstep.

# Dividend

Saturday, late morning, the fever began:
the short phone calls to the little man
that Aunty Bubbles knew, the form and weight
and starting price. "They're lined up at the gate
for the fourth at Victoria Park." The nasal voice
of the wireless galloped us fast as the winning horse.
"It's Valiant Boy by a short half-head."
"Oh pooh," our mother said, "another dud."

But when she wore her lucky hat to the races
once, her Uncle Clarry's grey, Sir Croesus,
came home on the rails at fifty to one.
He gave a pound note each to me and John,
and a taste for risk; we learned to back long shots,
dark horses, elderly relatives, and red hats.

# Stained Glass

At our grandparents', on the hottest days,
the leather sofa was cool; across our knees
was Grimm's in green and gold from the glass bookcase,
with Hans, Snow White, Falada, Little Claus,
slain children, witches, wolves, and hacked-off toes.
Prickling, we read at the empty end of the house
which breathed and waited; we sensed the slightest noise

and thought of the sun, the green and welcoming trees.
The dark hall curtains clutched to stifle us.
"More haste!" called Gran. Into the shining daze
we burst, and raced to the latticed summer-house
whose blue and green and red and yellow glass
made other worlds. We pressed our faces close
to the panes and entered each brooding paradise.

# Planting Seeds

He came back with a heavy limp
and a passion for growing flowers,
those fleeting colours close to the soil:
petunias, daisies, phlox,
the sharp beaks of strelitzia,
air's lace — gypsophila,
ranunculus, zinnias, stocks.
Early, we learnt their names
and how to tip streams of seeds
from split dried pods;
no packets for him,
he oversaw each season's safe return.
He'd round his palm
for the rattle of tiny money
from the pansy's three-way purse
then carefully plant out transience again.
Working with earth there was much he could forget.
But we were fierce to know —
*Daddy, tell us about the War!*
Sometimes he did — the action, rituals, names,
but feelings, never.
Stoical, he ground those memories down
with the bad leg's pain.
Except for that preliminary, half-aside;
he told it every time.
*As the Lancaster engines rose to a roar at dusk*
*they were always there,*
*in snow, in sleet, in rain,*
*a little group by the caravan at the runway's end,*
*old men and young mess girls in grey,*
*gathered to wave each crew goodbye.*
I think now that his larkspurs and sweetpeas,
foxgloves and bluebells, always English flowers,

touched that recurring scene,
the unfailing strangers standing for home
each dangerous setting-out.
I think they were his return.

# The Outside Lavatory

The red-brick lav
by the toolshed and the tank
had a wide wooden seat painted brown
with a long drop under the central flap;
even in winter the seat was warm.
No bottom could ever match that hole
but no-one ever fell in.
It was good for Hidey or Sardines,
a quiet cry, or just to sit.
You could hear the maggies in the pine,
a barrow trundling past,
or the Siggs boys having a fight,
then the swing and click of a wire door,
"Okay Ben Dover." Slap, yelp, slap, yelp.
Upside down in every corner
daddy-long-legs hung
and a gecko sometimes came in under the tin.
You'd watch the hessian door sway in and out,
or read the squares of newspaper on string:
*Miss Evelyn Gault, charming in emerald green...*
*remanded to appear in the Central Court...*
wondering about carnal knowledge and crêpe de Chine,
while tired flies lobbed on your legs and clung.
The smell was warm and stale
and peacefully sad —
old sacking, paper, dust,
and the ghost of excrement past,
mixed with jasmine from the trellis outside.
The secret code to work the chain
was two fast, two slow, count three, HARD.
Before you pushed in past the sack,
you knocked on the tank with a stone.
"Ya CARNcummin!"
"I HAVtago!"
The sound of the water trembled on and on.

# Beetles
*Three-quarters of all living species are insects
and of these, sixty per cent are beetles*


God's dinky toys are beetles,
his very favourite game.
*Can you keep a secret?* they scuttle
in your closed palm.

*I see no evil*, say the round eyes,
the cutlery of their mouth-parts
folded, polite. Like clockwork mice
they tumble over, feeling for castanets.

Daredevils of flight, they hurtle, whirr, thud,
back to scurrier, plodder, still jewel,
fob-watch cases clicking shut
on a petticoat wisp, a loose shirt-tail.

I remember a Christmas beetle I wore
as a golden brooch over my heart,
trusting the slow cogs of its thought.
It preferred my hair.

Far south of possibility, John
found a glow-worm once in winter grass.
We had good eyesight then:
it signalled us in morse.

*Ladybird, ladybird, fly away home.*
The flying saucers would lift back
to the rose leaves and zinnia stems,
epidemics of orange and black.

So many: click beetles (teachers' delights),
stink bugs for putting down necks,

creatures with feelers, horns, and funny snouts,
moley ones under bark, black lurkers in cracks,

their museum cousins pinned to fame,
and the scarab hollowed away
by a team of ants in the time
it took to fly or pray.

It was about then I read
the priests of Amon-Ra would sell
scarab charms for the dead
so when each trembling soul

reached Osiris' Judgement Hall,
*Witness not against me, Oh my heart!*
inscribed on the charm, would level the scale
against the feather of Maat.

The Egyptian Room, dusty with ancient death,
showed us a swaddled shape, a scarab seal;
we misted the glass case with our breath
but could not fathom body or soul.

Years later, near the Nile, an urchin ran
for miles beside my bike
hawking bruise-purple scarabs, fake.
Real cockchafers whizzed from the cane.

Still I can't resist turning
any likely stone
for Scarabaeus — Resurrection — shining
bronze, gold, green.

# Gloves I Have Known

Almost human, they flew off down the years,
chewed fingertips waving farewell
singly or rolled in pairs,
little fists for Saint Vincent de Paul.

Sloughed skins, failed roles,
pulled on so often, flexed and smoothed,
they grew an aura, a sort of soul.
Smelling of camphor, they come at my call.

Black kid, ladies', steam-rollered flat,
from the dress-up drawer.
We'd shunt along in forties' heels,
our fingers flapping like bats.

Blue bunny-wool skated me into dreams —
Sonja, the Ice Princess;
crocheted cotton — a Sunday doll;
pink mittens (knitted by me!) with baggy thumbs.

Monday to Friday, five to sixteen,
schoolgirl grey, one usually lost;
Saturday mornings, the Dance of the Little Swans
in see-through nylon frilled at the wrist.

A ladylike pair for the interview,
almost passé by then,
and these keepsakes in a flowered box,
elbow-length oyster satin. Pretty things outgrown.

# Loquats and Lacquerware

They flourished beside the clothes line or the tank
and shaded the dunnies on dry farms,
a sweetness between the leathery skin and glossy stones
like the slow smiles of the women near Goyder's Line,
pioneers, laconic survivors, lit up by fruit or rain.

Dour trees of Grandma's time, they claimed
the possums, birds, and neighbourhood kids
plumbing half-light to suck the pale flesh,
spit slippery pips and clang them on next-door's tin.
Drained skins the colour of summer lit the ground.

On Great Aunt's lacquerware box, a stream, a bridge,
	a tree —
*luh kwat:* Chinese rush orange. Under the lid,
a topaz brooch, seed pearls, a garnet ring.
Down the hall, footsteps coming. Click shut quick!
(A swirl of spit on the top lit the cowlicks to bright jade.)

# Old Soldiers

When the old soldiers
with their wisps of paper
more real than flowers
came up one by one
to lay the pale flames down
on the glowing wood
and stand, grey-suited,
still as the forty years gone,
a feeling quiet as petals,
faint as history thinning away
passed over us all.
Their breathing was a balancing out
of rank and medal and blood,
the orange terror in the sky,
and the clutched hand.
My father had spoken
little of that time
when he returned
so a man I knew and never knew
had died.
I glimpsed him in their faces
and spare gestures,
talking together afterwards outside.

# Touchdown

So it comes to me now,
this small gold grub with ruby eyes,
its owner finally down
after a lonely fall —
Flight Sergeant J.B. Sincock,
a member of the Caterpillar Club,
having saved his life by parachute.
I trace the pin latched on blue velvet
and think of the young rear-gunner, Vern —
Vern Scheldt, twenty, who did not quite
qualify for the Club
but lived with us ever after
in a frame on the mantelpiece.
I was five years old
when his mother and sister came with gifts,
the portrait and a lilac poetry book.
Every Sunday as I read,
his face looked wistfully down at me,
changing with the years
from my father's friend
to a fair young man,
a youth, a boy,
then my lost counterpart.
Today he could be my son.
Little remains — his smile,
remembered rhymes,
a rush of space to cross.
Now a single thought encompasses them
both safe down.
All distance closes in the end.
Already as I reach out, Vern,
I can almost touch your hand.

# Day Trip

The carriage shudders and rolls, no getting off
the illusion of stasis, of safety.
From the window seat a woman smiles.
She's nursing a baby from Vietnam
with a harelip like her own.
The baby will not smile. She stares
from eyes like two dark seas
till rocked to sleep. The angel hovering
in the corner there knows nothing of this,
trapped in perfection with so much to learn —
blood, war, healing, how to hold a child.
Here in second class we're sure of less and less.
Forgetting, as the train rocks on,
we watch the dust motes drifting in the sun.

# Group Portrait with Fireworks

If this jetty were fate we'd be done for,
circling the oysters and champagne on planks

that narrow into night — the first fist of dark,
a sketch by Munch or Magritte. Wind herds a blur;

tribal, we shamble, uneasily watching for fire.
Starboard the rockets wait, blatant with purpose

then spit sudden malice, thud vertigo through us,
fountain and flower. Gasps ebb with the light.

Tide is more constant, sloshing under our feet
swayed by the black no-moon, her seas blotted out.

Words sputter here and there, music and laughter
twinkle across the water, calling us in.

We look back from the shore; the jetty's bare,
a finger on emptiness — the Buddha sign.

# Mortgage

Years ago, to own a debt, the deed
was divided up — a zigzag tear was made
so only a perfect match would mean
the ragged halves had once been one,
such edges were impossible to fake.
I think of two old notaries in black,
peering to fit the pieces and redeem our land.

Remember, we could never find
the last piece of the child's jigsaw?
But metaphors will only go so far,
imperfect matches we give up:
the traveller is not the map,
deed is a stone of a word, divorce
wants to be final too, flashes like scissors.

# Level Crossing

An old man on crutches was crossing the road
with a bucket of coal from Ryan's Woodyard,

in long easy arcs so the bucket slung
from the hook on his left thigh stump jauntily swang

to counter each step as Newton proved it should.
And why should such a sight have made me sad?

It had flair, it had sprawl, his face wore the hint
of a smile, and the bucket was red. It clanked as he leant

to leap the kerb and leave us all behind.
The rhythm of it comes and goes in the mind

like breathing — the crutches, the foot, the swing
of the bucket, the crutches, the foot, the swing...

We cross that way too, with or against the lights,
lugging tomorrow's fire on any makeshift thoughts.

# Rheomode
*for Andrew Sant*


Late afternoon, we lean on the sill
over a city of birds.
The implicate order folds and unfolds
an origami of doves and leaves.
Through winter sun and traffic noise
improbabilities take wing —
pigeons, a toss-up of alms
for the scattering matrix theory,
sparrows' hyperbolas prove heaven,
and a mallard's splash-down
centres the universe.
"You were saying?"
"God knows!"
Another wave function collapses.
Over the road, without even trying,
light from a hundred million miles
goes on alighting
on the grey tower of Scots Uniting.

# EARTH-STAR

# Morning Song

The cricket's chirr    the mopoke's name
blur into miles of silent dream
till wattle-bird nags dawn with its ratchet throat
and wrens untangle their tiny cries    Daylight
and the acupuncture of sound begins
cough sigh shuffle clink bark whine
scritch    the phut and whirr of gas
miaows at the door    two cars whish past
little voices of iron snap and tick
jasmine rubs at the pane    wood creaks
tap makes a spare haiku    *tlip dlip pling*
then gushes chaos    fridge throbs igloo songs
coffee pot burps and hisses    extrovert
November day    espresso    hot    and sweet

# Red Carnations

Extravagance of red on spindle stems,
theatrical flourishes at passing time,
they burst like wounds of light. The one sleek bud,
a chrysalis of jade, is tipped with blood.
Butterflies, big spenders, thriving on praise,
they cool their fiery taffeta in a crystal vase,
flounce and swish a froth of skirts.
Listen — hand-claps, the snap of castanets,
drumming of heels, the zing of a guitar.
And yet they give, transcending all demands,
this edge of ecstasy becoming air —
perfume that draws on memory's fixed bonds
but squanders the profit just elsewhere.

# Fungus

Something dead and rotting, I thought,
chewed over by autumn and spat out
but a sponge of root grips as I tear,
lifts with a stink and a puff of spore -
dust, black smut from the open cup's
brown leather. Seven ragged scraps,
failed petals, neither flower nor mould —
the stuff of compost heaps — are curled
away from an empty eye, an obscene
smell almost animal, almost kin.
What's it good for? A certain cure
for warts, whitlows, and falling hair?
And what's it called? Ghoul's-balm, foul-strife,
witchbane, stenchwort, death-in-life?
"Fungi of Australia" lists its name;
I weigh it up: Earth-star: light in the palm.

# Blackberries and Walnuts

The last blackberries are soft
and dusty, utterly sweet.
Lichen shows through the hawthorn leaves,
a crow's caw creaks shut.

Everywhere, millipedes criss-cross the soil,
a plague of serpents, seen from a height,
no — runaway Italian express trains.
Crash! One's an ammonite.

The plane leaves are burst paper bags.
You can't philosophise
safely under the walnut tree —
nuts fall like tortoises.

A skink is sudden thought
spurting over a stone.
Both light up, mica, copper,
briefly precious in thin sun.

There's a Japanese word for all this —
the mint and leaf-mould feeding the air,
the honey-ant grapes along the verandah.
I reach down a bunch. The old dog waits for his share.

# Trees

## *The Rowan to Dance*

Twelve saplings to be planted out, the chosen
virtues for a south-facing garden:

the rowan to dance, a young girl ruby-decked,
the pussy willow's upright thrusts, smooth talk,

red and white dogwood so even leaves may flower,
wattle and banksia for birds, fast claimers of air,

laburnum since she weeps bright golden tears,
the corkscrew willow for his eccentric ways,

the lemon-scented gum whom nakedness clothes,
ash and maple whose bravest colours are death's,

a cherry tree to make a spring snowfall
and lilac for her sweetest breath of all.

## *The Cherry Tree*

They are planting the cherry tree on the slope,
dark loam grows to a soft mound on one side,
from here he could be digging a tiny grave.
The boy and girl are solemn, looking down.
She shakes the sapling loose and holds it clear,
the roots clutch downward, three red prongs
make a trident toward Aldinga Bay.
She lowers it in, he fills, she tamps it down.
Then round and round, holding the central stem,
she and her brother stamp in turn,
a lame dance round a bare maypole.

It is done. They stand as still as the little tree
at just that distance, whether of time or space,
that makes things formal and mysterious.

## *The Red Gum*

Hobby horses, wooden ducks and boats,
shanghais and stilts, trees gave, and cricket bats.
We thought of wings and jumped from trees to try;
they were the only climbing place of sky.

We'd squeeze inside a gum to hide —
time was crumbling the heartwood:
the leaves sighed *Where?* the hollow answered *Here*.
We held our breath: death never found us there.

That last shape as narrow as a cot,
sudden as the night-light out,
trees also give — a humble cradling power
down into earth, upward into air.

## *Smoke*

Trees cry as they fall *This is my body given for you*.
Old carpenters and cabinet-makers know
wood by its scent as lovers know loved skin.
Beyond the moving crests of gums and pines
over three valleys light-blue smoke is high-
rising from hidden homes to ghost the sky.

Someone is filling the middle air
with the two-note breathy music of the saw
that shapes the flesh of the tree for building or burning.
Our timber walls complain at the day's turning:
a log rolls over, the fire spits and purrs on,
wood and flames talking quietly of the sun.

# Calendar
*After Les Très Riches Heures du Duc de Berry*

*The Duke of Berry's hourbook, now in the Musée Condé at Chantilly, opens with a calendar; in most months either the Duke or one of his castles is featured. John of France, Duke of Berry, was a shrewd rapacious man disliked by the peasants, whom he exploited. His saving grace was a love of beauty. About 1410 he commissioned the Limbourg brothers, Pol, Hermant, and Jean, to produce the illuminated miniatures of* Les Très Riches Heures. *In 1416 the Duke and the three brothers all died; the incomplete work was finished by Jean Colombe and others some time before 1486.*

### *January     Feasting*

"Make January blaze at carrion cold,"
I said. "Be lavish with silver and gold —
plates, tankards, tapestries, and courtiers with gifts.
*Approach*, I'd have the central figure say —
I, John of Berry, at table in the Great Hall,
and paint yourselves, good sirs, among the crowd."
There's Hermant swigging down my ale.
Jean flatters me much less — pug nose, heavy jowl,
and wintry smile. He sees me clear,
a skill for which I pay him well.
Why should I, thick-fingered, plain, a practical man,
commission such a work? And at such cost?
(So soon the amaranth robe draws back your gaze!)
As a child I feared my room at night,
those dank grey walls at Vincennes closing in.
Our mother, Bonne of Luxembourg, would pawn
her jewellery and gowns to pay our debts;
she died of the pestilence when I was nine.
I turned against the dark, the ugliness, the end;
learned my limits: *Le temps viendra*. My choice,
not power like Louis, or learning like Charles,
nor glory like our brother, Philip the Bold.
Pleasure and treasure, I seized on.

But guile and greed serve beauty well,
plunder and bribes can be refined.
Art not alchemy transmutes such gold —
the perfect crafting of this swan and bear,
these endlessly unfolding *Très Riches Heures*.
What will your eyes find to blame or shun
tomorrow in the heavens shimmering here?

## *February    Fire and Snow*

Over the hills, haystacks, and hives,
over the village, wood, and pen,
snow has administered unction,
forgiveness of venial sins.
Precise, austere, it sits
in the crook of each tree,
on the upper rush plait of the fence,
clings to the wheel-rim top,
thins along the shafts.
There is a grey donkey for humility,
a woodcutter slicing the icy air for diligence,
and the farmer and his wife in the little house,
smocks drawn up, warm cock and quim at the hearth
with the gentle smiles of innocence.
The lady, their mistress, averts her gaze,
raises her blue robe just calf-high,
modesty talking to a cat.
A knot of magpies peck and wait.
The sheep make a sheltered huddle, warm
as the six legs stretched to the flames.

## *March    Pruning the Vines*

A Limbourg brother, the Courtly one,
painted the black fists of the vines
and the winged serpent of gold hovering over
the spire of Lusignan's russet-tiled tower —
one of the forms of the fairy Melusine.
Beyond the oxen lowering their lute horns

and the peasant at the plough, giant-size,
is something new — a darkness over the furrows —
the Master of the Shadows' daring hand,
though by the small crossroads a mountjoy stands
casting no shade. Puzzled you look again —
the soft-muzzled yellow ox is perfectly done
except... both right legs forward on its course,
the beast plods onward like a pacing horse.

## *April   Picking Flowers*
*Translated from the French of Charles d'Orléans (1391–1465)*

Time's tossed aside his shabby coat
of cold and wind and rain
to sport embroidery again
in sparkling April's clear sunlight.
Not a bird or beast stays mute,
each tongues and sings as best it can:
Time's tossed aside his shabby coat
of cold and wind and rain.

Spring and stream and brook are bright-
ly decked out in fresh livery —
silver drops, gold filigree.
Everyone's in their finery.
Time's tossed aside his shabby coat.

## *May ˙  Horse-riding*

Beyond the twisted wood
enchanted as Brocéliande,
the turrets of the Conciergerie
lift gilded flags, crosses and fleurs-de-lis.
*Buisine*, trombone, and three flutes go before
a jaunty cavalcade of youths and girls
with rose-leaf garlands in their hair.
The horses frisk, the Duke's two spaniels bark,
a shrill wild music summons the blood like sap.
Oh, to be a beardless troubadour!

The vibrance of brocade and silk
in richly indolent folds
celebrate May as if there never were
pox and leprosy and plague
black shillings under the arm,
a third of Europe dead,
till no-one wept and no bells tolled
*(And I, Angolo di Tura, called the Fat,*
*buried my five children with my own hands);*
the end of the world, they said.
As through the merest arrow slit,
narrow as safety in a castle wall,
behold a green and savage time,
deeds of chivalry and courtly love
flanked by torture, famine, poison, war,
north-west of romance, outside the frame.


## *June     Haymaking*

Three sunburnt reapers in a line
scything light-  out of dark-green
pattern the field below the walls
and azure roofs; like waterfalls
thirteen sturdily polled planes
surge new growth along the Seine.
The water ripples, mud-coloured, pale
as the swimmers and the barefoot girls
winnowing hay with rake and fork:
glean that curving quizzical look
that cuts a swathe between the two —
something unsaid. Beyond, the view
is dogma-solid: the Sainte-Chapelle to prove
time was; easier to believe
those bare legs and tucked-up skirts,
the rising scent of grass and sweat,
the to-ing and fro-ing, here and there,
that guarded secret in the air.

## July    Harvesting and Shearing

Bulrushes curve in the River Clain,
a narrow stream one step across;
the willow trees are smaller than the men;
shorn wool, a cumulus on the grass,
airier than the clouds of woolly gilt,
piles up between the sweet-faced sheep
and the blue-robed shearers in black hats.
Across the Clain two peasants reap
cornflowers and poppies with the wheat.
The Duke's proud emblem, two white swans,
sail the grey moat in noonday heat.
Of those white towers and ramparts, nothing remains.

## August    Hawking

The noble on the leading horse
frees his falcon's jesses and she's cast
to tower above the suddenly hushed hedgerows.
A coney panics from the corn,
two ducks break cover. "She's stooping, Sire."

Pupil widening on a yellow field,
she drinks in light, her shadow bursts, she kills
("Ho, my beauty. Come, bird.")
then lifts on the finest creance, trust
to perch on a gloved fist.

The swivel of the ladies' necks,
the merlin rousing on a wrist —
slight signs call us in, cast us away,
free, not free, over a field
that owns no quarry or prey.

## September    Gathering Grapes
*Translated from the French of Jean Molinet (1435–1507)*

This Paris wine's the first and best;
it's brimful of the Holy Ghost;

whoever tastes it long and well
knows good and evil, heaven and hell;
he sees the angels in their bliss;
he shudders at the dread abyss;
he meets his Saviour face to face;
he finds all power and wisdom his.
Because it hones the spirit fine
theology calls it divine.
Doctor, orator, and jurist,
teacher too, tanked, sozzled, pissed,
toss off by the pitcherful
a wine that blesses every meal.
Not for gourmands with faint hearts
and languid dainty appetites,
this wine preserved by skill and grace
in Athens, its first nurturing place,
was cultivated next in Rome
whence Charlemagne brought the root-stocks home
to Paris, city of renown.
Today we claim it as our own.

## *October   Sowing*

The fine brush barely touches the scene,
daring the unreal, shadows again,
burnt sienna over the ochre earth.
Two children lean in close
sucking on crusts of bread.
André swipes his runny nose,
"Look, there's François. And M. Légoux' horse."
"Dragin?" says Antoine, "Dragin?" Not a sign.
Pol de Limbourg sighs, "What's this?"
(Five deft strokes.) "It's Peloton!"
(Five more.) "And Louche!" Two skinny dogs
rampant under the battlements of the Louvre.
"And that, Monsieur?"
"A stone to keep the harrow down."
"But why is François sad?"
"He's tired."

"Well why do you let those birds peck up his seed?"
No answer. Rinse, dab, rinse.
Antoine tries his tongue to a dripping rim —
a glug as the full pot hits the floor.
"*Merde*," says the man and stoops
to the blue lake over the slate:
ultramarine for the scarecrow's coat.
An autumn afternoon, 1415,
purple seeping over the sill,
indigo deepening the room.

## *November    Harvesting Acorns*

This is the moment before the wielded stick
is hurled to thwack the nearest oak
and shake a rain of acorns on the backs
of Wurzel and Bristlebum who'll oink
as the old dog nips their rumps and hocks.
Then Jacques of the stick will narrow his eyes
at the distant blue between the trees —
a haze of smoke: the Companies are abroad —
d'Aubrecicourt and Calveley; he's heard
talk of another Crusade in Spain — pray God
it leech away these brigands like bad blood.
His pigs are a cheerful lot with turned-up snouts
and greedy smiles, rooting in mulch and dirt.
They grovel like penitents, Franciscan-brown,
fat with the shady-gotten gains
of hawking relics in market towns,
Moses' burning bush (a swatch of broom)
and Gabriel's feather (found in Mary's room).
Just pigs in the month of acorns; down they come
on Jacques and Wurzel and Bristlebum.

## *December    Hunting the Boar*
*Translated from the French of Eustache Deschamps (1346–1406)*

Each servant in the King's Household must stay
four months of every year at court, they say;

well there are four cold ones when I won't chance
my health in serving at the court of France —
from childhood on they've been too much for me:
November's one, December, January,
and February bringing ague and rheum:
in such cold weather better stay at home.

For then come frosts and rain and driving snow,
icy winds and gales begin to blow;
and when the King goes off to hunt the boar
his men slap at their sides in the chilly air
and blow their hands and wrap their cloaks around
their backs and bellies, stamping on the ground.
Horseback boys make faces full of gloom.
In such cold weather better stay at home.

The little snivelling pages cannot hold
the horses' bridles for the bitter cold;
God Himself would break out in cold sweat
at the lodgings and the meagre fuel doled out;
squires and servants with no cloaks at all
stand round stupefied in the dining hall.
Whoever hopes to miss this courtly game
in such cold weather better stay at home.

Prince or courtier with money enough
to cover these four months had best make off;
don't go to court for grievance or just claim:
in such cold weather better stay at home.

# CRYSTAL FORESTS

# Touchstone

## *Agates*

Crusty cannonballs
from prehistory
thunder eggs
round as Om
split
polished tame
make paperweights or clocks
Time looks wispy
half-ashamed
tracing millennial rings
dim as trachoma
Look here
a hollow at the core
has grown a crystal forest
of snow firs
the matched halves close
to a hairline crack
Inside
stone winds murmur
in stone trees
useless and wonderful
as Chinese toys

## *Malachite*

The name is the sound
of an ancient warlike tribe
steel against steel in mist
and the colour
a rumour of danger
rock-serpents
gryphons
green tigers

swirled on shields
Malachite
hung like crocodile tears
between damp breasts
dangling from earlobes
charms against a rival
or strung like milk-teeth
of a witch
trembling
on naked loins
See it fall
in the cauldron
to set the spell
stone of Circe
        Salome
                Jezebel

## *Amethyst Crystals*

Here in the field
of dragons' teeth
purple and indigo
geometry touches mysticism
remembering Vega's cities
of frozen music
Here the mineral kingdom
turns to the unknown
chemicals feel
for another form
stone grows
beginning
the slow ascent
to flesh
the deadly virus
cunning DNA
Half transparent
half opaque
these crystals float
a smoke of myrrh

the colour of exile
Admire their ground rules
facets and planes
clear as an angel's logic
no mirror for us there
These peaks though
press your palm down
implacable     alien     our own
the long thrust back
to the stars

*Fossil*

This fish won't stop swimming
through yellow mud
set hard
against the swimming
past bloodstream
hand and page
past metaphor of fate
still swimming
minus a tail     an eye     a fin
and all its wits
swimming
This fish
in its womb of shale
seven inches long     convex
left side exposed
keeps swimming
mouthed arrowhead
dead weight
dead ahead
Cretaceous to never
give up
still swimming
Touch
glass gills
diamond-scaled terrain
the etched gem of the belly

swimming
Towards a leap     a word
one wish
out of time
with the swimming
this fish
the stone ghost
of its smile
keeps on swimming

## *Tektites*

Droplets of siliceous glass
a mystery
tears of the moon?
space bilge?
devils' dice?
Territorial     we stake our claim
australites
black shapes of alien grief
or poker chips and tiddly-winks
a cosmic game
Compute     compute
orbital disintegration pattern
Origin     Copernicus B
Origin     Clavius A
Origin     Unknown
They stream past CETI's* coded plea
*Tell us we are not alone*
little enigmas strewn
like fossil raindrops over
the Nullarbor Plain

---

*CETI: Communication with Extraterrestrial Intelligence (US Space Program)

# Footprints
*Part of a large trackway recording the stampede of a
herd of small dinosaurs* SOUTH AUSTRALIAN MUSEUM

The one huge footprint is not shown
just these chicken feet fanning out
a patch of clover     splayed cuneiform
every angle of panic caught
in ochre mud     *I fear*     *I fear*
stamped over and over     the oldest sign
Driven beyond themselves they claw
icily up and down the spine
Shiver and look back     sensing how
a ravenous smile thunders along the track
This fierce yesterday is now
a pungence in the quiet museum's half-dark

# More on the Dinosaur

No wonder they almost died out,
with one full minute between stubbed tail and ouch,
their logic couldn't connect cause and effect.
Sex was an enigma — buoyed up in the mire,
cryptogams fringing their jaws
and their little eyes glassy with time-lag,
they'd quite forget, between effort and ecstasy,
just what they were at
(the other already wallowing off).
Imagine the bliss of brontosaurs —
embracing a mountain, incurring an earthquake —
love as a natural disaster.
But the urge to survive went deep,
they're with us still, in hindbrain, basal ganglion,
sometimes a stranger's eyes, and always
man's hidden part, blunt id,
barbed as the collared head of Triceratops,
a tip on tomorrow's winner.

# Fern

The idea of the shadow of a fern
caught in grey shale, a crosier's lean
scepticism, fingerprints on light,
have kept a century arguing half the night,

rifling the long memory of stone
whose finest thinkers filter down
from outer time's thin crust
green hypotheses of leaf and wrist.

Death's emanations they half understand —
a patterned lack of rock, absent ground,
but only the far-out theorists, sand and loam,
hold being is the horizon of time.

The molten centre seething on and on
shapes solid earth and draws it down again:
a dark relentless will to learn
the idea of the shadow of a fern.

# PATHWAYS

# Write to Me at Rochefort

*On 1 August 1785 two French frigates, the* Boussole *and the* Astrolabe, *set out from Brest on a voyage of discovery in the Pacific. The expedition was led by Jean-François Galaup, Comte de Lapérouse. At Maouna Island in December 1787, twelve of his men were massacred by natives. Scurvy was rife.*


Emerald    silver    sapphire    the spectra of paradise
rank with danger    vermilion-blue    blood-green
wind    waves    salt as Gomorrah
a gibbous moon    fish-white    floating

David becomes mapmaker and map
drifts toward the horizon
jettisons all instruments of navigation
memory    speech
dips over the edge of the world
knife    ladle    colander    pan
hang clean on the wall
The gulls discover a cruel joke
the door of the galley opens
shuts    opens    shuts
the eye of a sea-bird picking at thought

Approaching the Isle of Traitors
Father Receveur cradles his eye-patch
an ominous throb that hammers the silence in

South-west through heavy seas
the *Boussole* and the *Astrolabe* plunge on
a rush of foam    fish    star    white air
tasting of tomorrow
At night from the deck Jean-François watches
the phosphors colour the water
sinuous couplings
cold hell-fires for a solitary man

Against the lantern light his fingers flame
dark smooths the fate-line out

## *Jean François de Lapérouse*

Three days becalmed beside this rock, Pylstaart.
The small satisfaction of correcting Cook:
we place it four miles further north.
The men are dispirited and weak;
as Dagelet says this is the hardest time.
I've ordered extra rations of brandy and rum
and had the pigs killed:
Rollin and Lavaux believe the scurvy's at bay.
I fear you will hardly know me, Eléonore —
toothless, my hair quite gone.
This stillness makes our separation cut
like Rollin's knife, the least of winds
as influential a friend as La Marquise.
Waiting, I think more heavily on de Langle
and all the men lost, the boy so young.
The nights are clear and sweet,
sharp with alien stars;
Dagelet up past the midnight watch
with spyglass and lamp and chart.
Yesterday we watched a school of dolphins sport,
the watery light shining along their skin.
Suddenly, I thought of you.
I have from the Abbé some coral for a necklace —
he assures me, of the finest sort.

## *Eléonore de Lapérouse*

So, Dear Jean, I have embarked
on a most ambitious scheme:
no less than twelve seat-covers worked
in petit point. A fine pastime

pricking at silk with green and blue

(the scene is of a ship with flying fish
and dolphins) when I might have been with you.
It is black winter here. Indeed I wish

I had made shift to do as that Comtesse
who stowed away on board
her husband's vessel in the dress
of a cabin boy. Alas, instead

I needs must fashion tritons blowing horns —
their tails are most prodigious hard to do.
Tante Élise insists I must design
a mermaid on a rock for you.

That I will not. And the Abbé is not to bring
such curiosities back, my Love!
After supper every night I sing
that song you like about the turtle-dove.

## *Lapérouse*

A wind at last! South-west through heavy seas
to Norfolk Island; Collignon and La Martinière
solicitous to go ashore for plants and seeds
but everywhere, steep cliffs and angry breakers.
Clonard thought best to take no risk and I agreed.
So — back to the endless books and cards,
the dice games on the deck:
for a sou against boredom our men stake their shirts.
A diversion on the *Astrolabe* — fire
blazed up in Receveur's acid salts,
luckily soon put out.
Then, this morning, the sign that sets
them laying bets for shore:
the mewing and crying of sea-birds,
a multitude of them circling overhead.

January 23rd: a coastline thirty miles away.
We tacked to turn the cape,

a north wind blowing hard,
and before us — the British Squadron in Botany Bay.

## *Eora Tribe*

Swaying tall they come
walking tall
dark at the edge of the sky
dark on the water
high branches petalled white
moving this way     that way
like Yarranaby dancing clouds
like Yarranaby dancing rain
like the clan of the White Cockatoo     *Gareway*
shaking their wings like this     like this
to *Jujabala*     the Camp of Cutting-Down-Trees


## *Arthur Phillip and Henry Ball*

Lieutenant Henry Ball reporting, Sir.
Sit down, Lieutenant, sit down.
So. Did you manage to ascertain
who our unexpected visitors are?

Certainly neither Dutch nor English, Sir.
One wears a chef d'escadres pennant. We made out
only that the field of their flag is white:
they're offshore just too far.

The French on discoveries, as I thought.
Is this not a most extraordinary chance?
We shall discern the golden lilies of France
by tomorrow, I make no doubt.

We must press on without delay.
But first we'll wet our throats —
this French brandy's appropriate —
then tell Hunter we'll need the *Spy*.

## *Thomas Bryant (convict)*

Southward off Cape Solander
  Jack heard the sailors say:
Two of 'em tacking round the Point
  And into Botany Bay.

"Supplies?" I guessed. "No fear," says Jack,
  "It's the Dutch out for a fight,
Or Spanish pirates, or war broken out
  With the French. Either way we rot."

"No news is good for the likes of us."
  He pressed his ear to the wood.
"They're weighing anchor...hoisting sail.
  We're bolting, Tom, my lad."

Next day, but, we're out of that hole
  And a-cutting of trees. Says Jack:
"They was Frogs — with luck we could stow aboard
  And work our passage back."

"After the chats and weevils and dark?
  You're barmy, Jack," I said.
"Better stay on dry land and be
  A Government man instead."

## *Lapérouse*

Imagine our impatience, Eléonore;
all Europeans are countrymen
at such a distance from home.
On the 26th we let the anchor down
in seven fathoms on a bottom of grey sand.
A Lieutenant from the *Sirius* came aboard
confirming the Kamchatka news.
Their Commodore Phillip had sailed the previous day
seeking a more commodious place:
the Lieutenant made some mystery of his plans
(his crew did not!), I sensed a certain unease.

They could offer only "good wishes for our success".
I despatched Clonard to reassure and explain
our needs were few and such
as we could not fail of in this Bay.
We have put up tents and a stockade,
have two longboats in frame
and a plenitude of water and wood.
Dagelet fixes the latitude
at 33° 59' 1"

Lieutenants Dawes and King came yesterday to dine,
M. King, quite fluent in French, an amiable man.
They are settled at Port Jackson, 10 miles north,
with upwards of 700 convicts, supplies not ample, I guess.
I should like to meet this Commodore Phillip
but not to change places with him, I confess.

*Philip Gidley King (Diary)*
*February 1st, 1788*

2 in y$^e$ morning sett off in a Cutter for Botany Bay
To visit Monsieur De La perouse, obliged to row all y$^e$ way

Arrived at 10 o'clock in y$^e$ Morning
Received with the utmost politeness and attention

Monsieur de la perouse having Stores &c enough
Offered to oblige M$^r$ Phillip with any he might want

As y$^e$ wind came on to blow fresh from y$^e$ Northward
Consented to dine with y$^e$ French Commodore

I found he had been at y$^e$ following places viz.
Madeira, Teneriffe, S$^{ta}$ Catherina

Y$^e$ coasts of Chile & California
Kamschatka where he replaced the Inscription

Near Capt. Clerke's Grave for which I thanked him
Macao, y$^e$ Phillipines, Sandwich Islands

Isles des Navigateurs, Friendly and Norfolk Islands
At Maouna he lost Monsieur De langle

8 Officers, 4 Men & 1 Boy, massaccred
By the natives, besides a great number wounded

Each Ship has 3 Time keepers hung on gimbals by Berthand
They have also a dipping needle which was with Cook

Monsieur De La perouse informed me he had found
All y$^e$ works of Captain Cook to be very exact and true

An Abbé also on the expedition
Appears a Man of Letters & Geniality

Next Morning at 5 took our leave, obliged to row all the way
Against the wind  Onboard y$^e$ Sirius 7 in y$^e$ Evening

## *Father Joseph Receveur*

I shall lie here in the sun, watching the men:
Joseph and Jean sowing carrots and beans,

the Abbé leaping off again with his net,
grasshopper hunting grasshoppers — a sight

to provoke the Indians. Ah, Boutin sees
and sends a guard. Always through the trees

I sense the darkness of their skin,
those white streaks like dancing bones

mocking and beckoning. How this land
conceals itself: neither takes the stranger's hand

nor rejects it quite — even the leaves
turn half-away, glittering more like waves

than foliage. And who would guess
flowers like brushes, a fox which flies,

rainbow-coloured birds, or know
truth from illusion regarding the kangourou?

The lines and colours here are strangely mute
or sharp, stark — an odd trick of the light —

as when near dawn you drift up through sleep's blur
to walk a territory trembling clear,

more real than real, and yet you know you dream.
*Diable!* These ants are real enough, it seems!

Back to my letter: *We shall be home*
*dear brother, by Spring of 89.*

*Write to me at Rochefort or at Brest.*


## *Lapérouse*

Am much cast down today, Eléonore:
quite suddenly Joseph Receveur
has died. He had made light of his wounds,
seemed in good spirits. His was a curious mind,
a patient heart. I lose another friend.

The longboats are almost complete,
still under constant guard —
the Indians would burn them if they could.
A number of the deserters have applied
most earnestly to come aboard:
we sent them on their way with water and food.

This is the last I write.
A Lieutenant Shortland will convey
our despatches to London —
the *Alexander* sails, I believe, in July.

From here I shall go up
to the Friendly Islands,
trust they deserve their name —
I am not as you know
of the philosophers' mind —
thence New Guinea, the Gulf of Carpentaria
and the west coast of New Holland
as far as Diemen's Land.

By Spring of 1789
we shall be home
My Dearest Love.


*On 10 March 1788 the* Boussole *and the* Astrolabe *sailed northward past Port Jackson. They were never seen again. For forty years their fate remained a mystery. In December 1827 Captain Peter Dillon reported evidence of their shipwreck on Vanikoro in the Santa Cruz Archipelago. In February 1828 Captain Dumont D'Urville found the remains of the frigates.*

## *Thomas Bryant*

December 5th the news got out:
    I'd called on Peg Molloy
For a bit of this and that — the *Gazette*
    On the table caught my eye.

I gave it a cross-eyed lawyer's squint,
    And was off like a knacker's hack
To the *Fox and Hounds* on Castlereagh Street,
    "Remember them French ships, Jack?"

". . .Initialled relics of Lapérouse,
   Captain Dillon reports.
Their shipwreck and subsequent demise
   Now seems in little doubt."

"A fleur-de-lis stamped jug was found,
   A few small bells," Jack read,
"A blacksmith's vice, (the men pushed round)
   A razor, an old sword blade."

"Grog's on the house," he called to Ann,
   "We'll drink to Lapérouse.
To the Frenchmen, lads, and all brave men
   Brought down by treacherous seas."

## *Eora Tribe*

Shaking their wings like this     like this
like the clan of *Gareway* shaking their wings
over the place of Sting-rays shaking their feathers
those people pale as the moon     *Yenadah*
folding their wings to the place of Sitting-Down
those people pale as bone
making the horns of *Yenadah* on their boughs
following running water     looking for food
calling the earth *boodjeri*
calling the fire *boodjeri*
resting by *Jujabala*
resting in the place of Making Canoes

# Hotel

Leicester Court was misrun
by five nationalities;
the shower was cold, the lift stalled,
and the key wouldn't turn.
On the second day I complained
and they sent the handyman up.
It was him again,
dark eyes and a soft moustache
too melancholy for anyone but a Pole.
The problem was not the key,
the lock was worn;
it worked three quarters in,
he showed me how.
"Please. You try,"
(his hand over mine):
the right fit, slight opposition,
an easing home,
and it opened sweet as a thought.
He nodded and smiled in that wry way
ideal and actual don't quite meet.
*And that's how you'd be. Yes.*
*Warm, sad-funny, precise,*
*with a sort of elusive grace*
*so even afterwards*
*telling when you were small*
*and the geese chased you up the cherry tree*
*on your uncle's farm,*
*you wouldn't be close,*
*the bed would be seven valleys wide,*
*distance would flute you away.*
It's a skill they learn in the Eastern bloc,
patching and fixing, making do;
also the indirect route, and the absence game.

I can't revert to third person singular now;
thank you dear second person singular Pole
for the knack; it worked like a charm.

# Metro

Buskers, somewhere at Châtelet —
their plainsong sounding the corridors for sky
raised transept, nave, and vault,
flooding them with unearthly light,
a silvery puzzlement the soul must feel,
roaming artery, neurone, bowel.
At Tuileries a small drunk man lurched on,
slumped down and breathed in my hair. The train's
precipitate birth hurled us along
a darkness beyond the reach of song.
"Un homme seul, tu comprends." I looked away
hoping he wouldn't vomit or cry.
"Tu comprends pas la solitude?"
He kept it up well past Concorde:
"English? I understand English. Look,"
he searched his coat for a paperback —
it was Gulliver clawing out at us
from the grip of a leering giantess.
He followed a black girl at L'Étoile
but missed the exit. I went up in the spill
of feet to a rush of wintry air
and the Champs Élysées plane trees sifting stars.
You could take wrong turns and trains for hours
down there — the labyrinth breeds on emptiness,
claims any outcast. Sometimes the choice is just
two different ways of being lost,
soul and seul are both importunate.
But I wish I'd smiled; these words come too late.

# Tower
*Tower of Belém, Lisbon*

We split the pomegranates in the sun
by the river's shifty sounds of grey —
ruby juice and bitter seeds gritty as shale.
In purdah of blue, the daylight moon peered down
as we reached the shimmering tower,
whitest filigree or a pillar of salt.
Years hollowed every step of the spiral stair
and each slit eye of the wind was aquamarine.
Tapestries shuddered and breathed
from the chilly walls, touching a chest, a chair,
on the little rounds of stony floor
where stiff-busked ladies paced and sewed,
slim fingers pricking out another world
in the prison of their century:
a May Day scene — hounds, horses, men,
headlong at their quarry, furiously free,
with wild flowers opening under the feet of the deer,
and high up on the azure, finely done,
a small white bird flying the other way.

# Town
*Eisenstadt, Austria*

The alliance was uneasy even then.
Close to the border
we found that day
your country as it was
before the war
renamed *Kismárton* Eisenstadt.
Arched doors and gateways, fruit trees,
angular houses, plain or baroque as clouds.
Eszterházy Palace where Haydn played,
and Liszt in the Square,
elegant even in stone.
In the little cake-shop where you bought
the cakes of your childhood,
*almás rétes, pózsónyi kifli,*
they spoke the old tongue still,
only you paid in schillings not in forint.
"*Köszönöm szépen,*" smiled the broad-cheeked woman.
The church was a simple dome,
a beehive of russet shadows and yellow light,
round and warm as a country stove,
homely enough for a child to believe in God.
The sky was open as the *Alföld*.
We sat on a wall to eat.
"Look."
A walnut tree by a barn, a wooden cart,
geese honking through wet grass
and an arc of rainbow in bruised light.
"Hungary."
You could not swallow,
staring along the fault-line of a dream.
Hungary. As close as we ever came.

# Kafenio
*The feast-day of Saint Matrona. Mitilene, Samos*

Ribbons, flowers, angel scraps,
*Kyrie eleison*
old women casting sidelong glances,
crossing and kneeling, not to be outdone,
*Khriste eleison*
candles weeping, a censer swung like time
bearing down the priest consumed by hidden flames
or the mouths of the children at his hands,
*Kyrie eleison*
his beard, crisp curling, wickedly lush.
Outside at last to the blessed sun,
the squat caressable cubes, the olive trees
and *kafenia* disgorging their shade to the east.
In one, the feast already underway
with a crush of bodies, taut handkerchiefs
circling high as Samos air or wine
and the tipsy bouzouki music reeling them in.
In the other, a stretch of deserted chairs,
at a table, three old men,
slack amber beads, the silence of *tavli*,
two playing, one looking on.
Spiros the barman had a sister in Melbourne —
the others nodded — a brother, three cousins, two sons:
"*Oli efygan*," said one, "all gone."
We drank ouzo and watched the board,
Spiros explained.
I couldn't follow the rules,
it seemed a dark game.

# Room
*Jerusalem*

A white hand-moulded cave,
alabaster in the heat:
a bed, a table, a chair.
The hubli-bubli in the hall
chuckled at Mohammad's jokes.
The roof looked over awnings
weighed with trash
to the desert-gold Damascus Gate,
streets of lamps, slung carcases, brocade,
and a gleaming-skinned old man
treading sesame seed in a churn.
Caged finches shrilled by doors;
a beggar felt along the stone,
his bowl spilled sun.
Coffee and oranges coloured the air
of the quiet room;
the narrow bed smelt of river water.
The walls are still
only a cubit out of reach,
calm as a lily,
plain as unrisen bread.

# Bridge
*Galata Bridge, Istanbul*

Under the arch in narrow boats,
little fish just caught
sizzled and browned in charcoal smoke,
a taste between heaven and earth
(wrapped in the pages of a telephone book).

We licked the last juice off our skin
and stepped into Asia, swallowed down
by squalid alleys, gold mosques, dirt and myrrh.
This bridge to this, an aromatic trace,
the sea taste of between, the almond taste of where.

# ZIPPERS

# Watching the Battle from Afar

What irks Xerxes?
Turks in Mercs
and maids in maxis
anachronistic Greeks in taxis
TV punk rock blue-jeaned jerks
quasars quarks and military perks
Star Wars Kleenex nylon socks
the CIA and swinging sex
Everything!
It sucks to be
twenty in 499 BC
Everything     fleet and phalanx
from tricky Greeks to high tech Yanks
Xerxes thinks that history wanks

# Domestibilia

### *Thimble*

Pocked silver donned
he levels the spear
his lady's blue silk ratifies the air

Third on the left
smoothing a fold
she bides her time in a chastity belt of gold

This game played at Bayeux
made sea-green horses shy
at gryphons     dragons     portents in the sky

### *Safety-pin*

So much depends
upon
a wide steel
buckle
glazed with chrome
snapped straps
nappies
zapped-out zippers
Cynics' togas
sceptics' slippers
Philistine morals
Spartan pride
the modesty of
Persian and Mede
Discreet retainer
of slave and king
through thick and thin
he holds his tongue

## *Zippers*

Landlocked xylophones
zippy metaphors for a metaphor
they hang in haberdashers'
smiles for sale
lightweight and heavy duty
or little toothy cunts
quaint as pirănha
Coupling chromosomes
their name's
a glad come-cry
One slip
and they're incompatible
millipedes out of sync
mute O
for a ménage à trois
with a sturdy safety-pin

## *Coat-hangers*

Their
    shoulders
        slump
to mobiles
    jemmies
        curettes
Naked
    they make
        complaining gamelan
"Where
    have all
        the florals gone?"
Robed
    they are
        silent queues
faceless
    going nowhere
        in the dark

# Alphabet

α   *Alpha* arrives
first fish or
egg with a claw
the clutch for ∞
falling being

β   *Beta* boozes
big-bellied bouncer
on a pogo stick
never loses
sportmanship prizes

π   *Pi* pirouettes
describes a circle
offers a maid a bed
constant as riddles
restless as blue fumes wreathing Venus

φ   *Phi* fibrillates
humming top
earth on its axis
yourself on your's
listen    the music of the spheres

χ   *Chi* connects
a kiss    a vote    a name
hope on a map
algebra resolved
the unknown soldier    home

ψ   *Psi* seems
Bohm's wave field
funny business on the syllabus
black tricks    bent forks
enduring as myth    certain as Triton

# Still Life with Coffee Pot
*After the painting by Vincent van Gogh*

Over the china a plump spout peers
past grey-blue shadows reaching to the right;
the solid things, like all his jugs and jars,
stream left, the side of silence, madness, art.

A black pot arabesques with heavy grace,
squat cups stretch vermilion rims,
a chequered milk jug grown elastic as chess,
leans beyond the litany of names.

These are the humble moved by a vague unrest,
handled shapes of light, dumb to be told.
The fruit sits tight, easy of any quest,
bright worlds of tangerine and gold.

# Pan-pipes

Round sadness     at the heart of things
the hollow core     an otherworld
in silver air     trembles to be
the formula     more distant than words

This is nothing     already known
reeds    irises     a water bird
brown hands     wild wind

By the door     crab-apple trees
Malus eleyi's     pagan cheek
Golden Hornet's     noon sun

# Saxophone

And what would Orpheus have thought
of you     dear clown
vulgar     innocent     wise
dreamed up by Mercury and Bacchus
you are the life of the party
doing impersonations after a beer
crying on someone's shoulder after two more
You roar     you croon     you belch     you groan
a whole barnyard moons in your belly
sad funny singer of the human heart
soulful as hippos mating     hopeless as drunks' alley
boisterous as a circus hitting town
Oh yakety sax when you come on
I have to smile
my knees and elbows jiggle     I bounce
I've afro curls     ebony skin
hips with ideas of their own
big with music     I dance